Krypton Nights

Winner of the Year 2001
Paris Review Prize in Poetry

Krypton Nights

Poems by Bryan D. Dietrich

Zoo Press

Zoo Press • P.O. Box 22990 • Lincoln, Nebraska 68542
Printed in the United States of America

Sponsored by *The Paris Review*
541 East 72nd Street • New York, New York 10021

Distributed to the trade by The University of Nebraska Press
Lincoln, Nebraska 68588 • www.nebraskapress.unl.edu

Cover design by Shelly Fraley © 2002

Additional design work, LeAnn Jensen

Library of Congress Cataloging-in-Publication Data

Dietrich, Bryan D.
  Krypton Nights / by Bryan D. Dietrich.— 1st ed.
    p. cm.
Year 2001 winner of the Paris Review Prize in Poetry.
  ISBN 1-932023-00-3 (alk. paper)
  1. Superman (Fictitious character)—Poetry. I. Title.
  PS3604.I37 K79 2002
  811.6—dc21
                                    2002012454

zoo011

First Edition

Acknowledgments

The author would like to thank the following journals in which some of these poems have appeared:

The Bellingham Review: "Through a Glass, Darkly"; *The Nation*: "Give to Her Your Cloak Also"; *The Paris Review*: "Behold the Man," "The Destruction of the Temple," "The Face of the Deep," "The Fourth Man in the Fire," "The Letter of the Law," "The Model," "The Theft of the Firstborn," and "The Trials of Job"; *Prairie Schooner*: "Man or Superman" and "Orgasm Over Mt. Ararat"; *Quarterly West*: "The End of Days," "Krypton Nights," "On Jephthah," "The Else," "JHVH," "The Mysteries of Azazel," and "The Curse of the Pharaohs."

Thanks to Writers at Work and Albert Goldbarth for awarding "The Jor-El Tapes" the 1996 Writers at Work Fellowship in Poetry. Thanks also to Linda Gregerson, Carl Phillips, Marie Ponsot, Grace Schulman, *The Nation* and the 92nd Street Y for awarding "Autobiography of a Cape" and "The Lois Lane Diaries" the 2001 "Discovery"/*The Nation* Award in Poetry.

Thanks to my father for introducing me to the Superman myth, to Jerome Siegel and Joe Shuster for "creating" it, DC Comics for perpetuating it, my sisters for preaching it to me, and my mother for putting up with it all.

Thanks to my many teachers, including Carol Short, Allen Harper, Callie Fieldcamp, the Oklahoma Summer Arts Institute, Dorothy Wiley, David Lollis, Jim Axley, Tyrone Wilkerson, Jane Shore, William Pitt Root, Andrew Salkey, Madeline DeFrees, Ingrid Shafer, Jerry Holt, Joseph Tuso,

Ric Baser, John Feaver, Bob Wernsman, Fritjof Capra, James Ragan, Hubert Selby, Jr., Arthur Vogelsang, James Grimshaw, Scott Simpkins, Giles Mitchell, James Tanner, Andrew Hudgins, Cynthia Macdonald, and Bruce Bond. Thanks also to the myriad friends along the way: Bobby Bowers, Jeff Fredrick, Bill Martin, Scott Miller, William Bohn, Michelle Willis, John McKenna (a promise kept), Rex Perkins, Rhonni DuBose, Marz Haglund, Albin Zotigh, Will Orr, Gail Sloop, Darla Lee, Rex Guinn, Brandon Case, Tony Hays, Shawn Sturgeon, Meg and Clint, Karen Love, Gail Pizzola, Deanna Zitterkopf, Drew Bogner, Greg Smith, Cheryl Golden, James Love, Philip Sueper, Aaron Leis, Essie Sappenfield, Jerome Stueart, Nathan Filbert, John Jenkinson, Lise Goett, Kerry Jones, the Harry's Uptown group, the Milton Center, Henry Taylor, and Neil Gaiman.

Particularly, I must thank Scott Cairns, mentor and friend; if it weren't for his class on Poetry as Midrash, this book would never have been started. And if it weren't for Alice Stewart, Curtis Shumaker, Tim Richardson, and Vicky Santiesteban, it would never have been finished. Also, thanks to Richard Howard, Neil Azevedo and Zoo Press for believing it should at last leave Kansas.

And finally, special thanks to John Jones, Dungeon Master, for salvaging the manuscript from an ancient and unreadable disk, to Shelly Fraley for providing it a handsome disguise, and to Gina Greenway for piloting it from suspicion to proof.

For my Father

Table of Contents

Autobiography of a Cape

The Jor-El Tapes

The Secret Diaries of Lois Lane

Lex Luthor's Complaint

A Note on Bryan Dietrich's *Krypton Nights*

For a poetry as convincing and accomplished as this, for a mythology as exhaustively researched, one looks for models, prototypes, antecedents, wondering where to plant the bars of the cage when the captive has been so cunning so long. The best I can come up with is Turner Cassity, our Klingsor of the Serials, who back in the eighties published a grim little jape on "The Southeastern Comic Book and Science Fiction Fair to be held in Atlanta," wherein the Enemy speaks thus to a deaf-mute in search of dog-eared Marvels:

> ...If I promise, I your Tempter,
>
> All the world and tights that never crease,
> How will you answer, dumb, Get thee behind me.
> You will not? Well, if you need to ease
> Clay feet, I shoe them. You know where to find me.

But Cassity requires the pathos of History, and of her wayward daughter Class Consciousness, for his poetical heartbreaks, and sends only this minor grimace in the direction of Superman and Co., a popular religious phantasmagoria which Dietrich has mined so deeply that it is only his garrulous deftness which keeps him from being the exhaustive Aquinas of the affair.

No, there is no antecedent High Versification in our theology of Comic Books, though we can immediately recognize the subject in its place and wonder why not? Perhaps because the stern stipulation for the Tinsel City of God is not only a proud and interplanetary imagination (Hollywood, Here We Come!) but a metaphysical sympathy I should expect to find only among the most loosely lapsed of Catholic readers—readers of *Superman Comics* as an epyllion to Dante's divine version.

When you're working with elements as "elementary" as the Lost Babe of Krypton, as crude, not to put too fine a point on it, as the Doomed Planet which has given its All, or its Best, to an analogously doomed Earth (do we not all feel?), it is Order that is the one thing needful, Device which must serve the turn, and Dietrich is of course wonderfully armed and outfitted with orders and devices of every kind, from Clark Kent's crown of seven sonnets climaxing in the inevitable Adam-to-Jesus muddle:

> ...for Clark, Superman, me: Fruit, fig-leaf, fakery,
> Coming home to a hard day's Gethsemane.

To Lex Luthor's wicked complaint from the Arkham Asylum:

> Should I lift a leaf from Lovecraft, from Poe?
> Explain, oh-so-lucidly, just what sort
> of mad I'm not? Tell you all the gorgeous
> things I've done were done for my father's sake...

And wiliest of all, the poet of *Krypton Nights* has taken the omnipresent dialogue of comic strips (even comic *books* are all talk, nothing *behind*) and made it too, even it, into a structural order which is the prosodic justice of his entire art. As Henry James once remarked on the exceptional use of talk for architectural [poetic] purposes, "really constructive dialogue, dialogue organic and dramatic, speaking for itself, representing and embodying substance and form, is among us an uncanny thing..." For Dietrich the thing is indeed uncanny, but so inveterate as to be—for his readers—only natural, only nurturing, only necessary:

> ...This is what we are,
> Not supermen, not perfection dressed
> in our garish red, blue and yellow Sunday

best. We, the world we read, are Torah.
Superman, the constancy of his concupiscent star,
is less than this. A big red S. A text
we read too lightly.

The author of *Krypton Nights* has made a remark-
able contribution to American literature: he has added
another scarlet letter to our alphabet of heroic undergoing,
and his "big red S" embellishes the breast of a fondly inter-
preted icon. Move over, Hester Prynne, make way for
Superman!

— Richard Howard

He thought according to the Law, spoke according to the Law, and did according to the Law; so that he was the holiest in all the living world, the best ruling in exercising rule, the brightest in brightness, and most glorious in glory, the most victorious in victory. And at his sight the demons rushed away.

—from the teachings of Zoroaster
The Zend-Avesta, 591 B.C.E.

Superman never made any money
For saving the world from Solomon Grundy
And sometimes I despair the world will never see
Another man like him

—Crash Test Dummies
The Ghosts That Haunt Me, 1991

I Kent

Listen, it isn't even my planet.
I just work here. A man of letters, mild
mannered, nerves of less than steel. Yes, I can
outrun most anything—thieves, mid-range sports
sedans, Shoemaker-Levy—can chew
a mouthful of coal to a cud of diamonds,
but I'm not as Delphic as you dream. I get
sleep apnea, hemorrhoids, runs in my tights.

I like Gilligan's Island and late night horror
flick medleys. Thermonuclear trust funds,
Greenpeace for guns, heavy metal milk lobbyists....
None of it gets me wet the way it used to.
If I could, I'd curl up in my cape
with an old comic, an orange soda,
a little Vivaldi. No telephone
booths, just Ming the Merciless to take me

away. Oh well. Shit happens. Worlds collide,
babes fall out of the sky, grow up, get lives.
My flat's just over there. No, the brownstone.
Yeah, that one. Corner room, third from— No. Up, up....
Anyway, I took this position because,
frankly, it looked like a job for me. Now
I'm not so sure anymore. I'm tired of being,
well, necessary. You don't know what it's like.

Hardly feeling a thing, seeing through
people, overhearing assassination plots
two countries over and still needing
new underwear every Christmas. One day
I hate the boots, belt, bikini, this S appliqué;

the next, I feel like punching every hornrimmed
dweeb I see. Dad warned me it might be like this.
"Son," he said, "you'll just wanna come home." Problem is,

I can't.

Autobiography of a Cape

A Crown of Sonnets by C. Kent

"Fair enough." Perry came around from behind his desk. "We all have a life outside these walls, and what you do with yours is none of my damn business…as long as it doesn't reflect badly on the Planet.*"*

—Roger Stern
The Death and Life of Superman, 1993

I. The Fourth Man in the Fire

Home from a hard day's Armageddon,
slipping out of spandex and into spectacles,
from one high life bold above the abandon
into another (shall we say less Pericles

than Prospero), I find that I suspect
this Superman I've become. Dressing down
is easier, the lie somehow less circumspect.
And though this *too* is dressing up, the clown

suit *cum* reporter's wardrobe boasts less blood
between the seams. I don't mind the dumbing
down, really. Being the neighborhood
god, all guts and gusto, well, it's numbing.

But here, just another byline for a vast news magnate,
I can stumble, fumble, fail. I can always quit the *Planet.*

II. The Trials of Job

I could stumble, fumble, fail, quit the planet,
head for the first unrehearsed star to the right
and then vanish, over lunch, say, some strange event
horizon. My alibi? Space frenzy. Airtight.

But, approaching omnipotence, where does one run?
I suppose I just feel torn sometimes, between
cape and capacity, between what I've done
and what you've *let* me do. The half seen

gestures of this politico, that pontiff,
the anchor's sly nod at half a hundred stations,
editors, my boss (most people, really, if
you want to know the truth), they, their nations,

whole parliaments have ratified me.
What happens, then, should I turn? Back toward eternity?

III. The Theft of the Firstborn

What happens then? Should I return, back toward
eternity? Start over, seek that old crabgrass orchard
deep in the Kansas scree and wait for my metal
cradle, the star that chose Pa's field, to settle?

Actually, it was all corn where my crib
came down, but if I *could* go back, trace time's rib
around to come out thirty years more whole
than any toddler, ostensibly, set before me; if I stole

myself from then, left only a smoking husk
behind; if I raised myself on some dead, dusk-
less world, that violet-blue one just off the edge of M31,
how, then, would I explain this suit to my "son"?

How define crest? How, without wars, Czars, rules?
On a field, yellow, the letter *S*, gules?

IV. The Letter of the Law

On a field of yellow, the letter S, gules.
This is how my parents found me, flames
cutting a swath across the farm road near the school's,
only stopping their red weave where the James'

property ended and Pa's began. The sign
my folks followed, then—that cosmic spoor
which led to a small blue craft cratered to the spine—
spelled not so much a warning as the future.

When my mother—unaware of the root
of her design (that red, ruthless curve)—stitched
something less letter than Kansas cornfield
to my chest, anchored me to my past, affixed

me to an arc dark as blood, was it heraldry or shield?
She and Pa still read the sky. I've tried to follow suit.

V. The Face of the Deep

My folks still read the sky I've tried to follow. The suit,
though, gets in the way of being human.
Even *being* human, stubbing one's foot,
say, or regretting the bloodletting of all but a few…. Man,

it's rough. There are times I've had to reset teeth, back
into laws I've broken myself, ensuring
some purer notion. Two selves then. Each a plank
for the other's platform; each, a hasty mooring.

Like some deranged Phoenician navigator
set adrift on theory molded mostly of the paper
he's penned his calculations on, I guess I find my taste
for figures growing thin. And how odd to waste

time hanging sky, when I'd rather be down
here anyway. Deep, where Superman may drown.

VI. The Destruction of the Temple

Here, anywhere, deep. Where Superman would drown.
Why even ask? Of course that would be untimely
for us both. So maybe I step into a ray gun,
one of Luthor's, burn away the steel. Finally

farm myself out to a sun that doesn't heal
so well. Or, what the hey, go ahead and steal
one of those Green Lantern rings, wish myself
no longer bird but plain. The thing is, your health

has depended on me, this antibody,
too long. And you would, I suspect, *still* see
me, bring me back like some dead, desert King,
refit me in his sequins. No, nothing

I can do, then, will relinquish me my cup.
These days I flee to where the ice is calving, cracking up.

VII. Behold the Man

These days I flee to where the ice is calving.
Where cracking up comes easier on reflection
of each high white embankment, each rose erection
the sun makes of glaciers here. This is where traveling

stops: Waste of iced barrow. Fortress of bone. Naked
Eden. Here, nature's choices have narrowed to death,
to survival of those too fit to be kind.
This is necessary, how we lie. When that Lord High Breath

came to Eve, demanding the source of the seed
on her thigh, He knew, of course, already.
For her, then, choice was not at all some rash, heady
option. Not till *after* the eating. Indeed,

it's the same for Clark, Superman, me. Fruit, fig leaf, fakery,
coming home to a hard day's Gethsemane.

The Jor-El Tapes

Transcripts of Binary Transmissions Recorded by the Very Large Array (Socorro, NM)— Originating in the Vicinity of Supernova 1993J.

Superman is a good cry; and a good cry is half the battle.

—George Bernard Shaw
Man and Superman, 1903

The End of Days

The end of your world will give you pause.
Not the tectonic euphoria
you might imagine: Streets suddenly filled
with a distaste for the horizontal.
Local shopkeepers, the odd dog, abrupt
and incandescent, breaking impossible laws.

Gravity comes to mind, occasional
looting. But not these either. Corpses,
their dusty bouquet. All, of course, miseries
I do not suggest you forget. But then
we are not engaged in exorcising
neighborhoods only, coastal metropoli,

myriad federal (if not eternal)
deficits; these, too, will go to whatever
ground is left more than a bit shaken.
No, the thing about a planet gone to gap
entirely, in toto—no stab
at reprieve—is that you still expect

so little from your salvation. A burial
spoon, an onyx spear, a monograph
on Galvanic law. A pair of shoes.
Any of these, the knowledge of their having been
left behind, would prepare you for your own
absence, the kind you are used to. You could live,

in other words, with the promise.

Krypton Nights

If I could leave my shadow only
behind, the air my body displaced
these many years, the suggestion
of water, night sweat, where just, say,
a cheekbone was before…. Dread. Even
that I would bequeath you if I could.

Yet, if you've received this, remember
tall sticks planted in the ground at noon.
No, remember there is no this. No
me. No reader, no last planetary
observer. No journal, no witness,
no conclave, no revival, no grand

revolution, no susurration,
no sea to come from, no sun to return
to, no Krypton days, no Krypton nights.
Only charmed figments of electric
residue. This ghost of light, pulse,
silence. Binary diaspora. This me

who I am not but will be soon, if only
briefly, until you turn toward your own
pale sun, the focus shifts, the quality
of light changes, and the shadow you
yourself cast grows shorter or longer
and you find that you've found another

me, and through me, another fragment
of who I may suggest, and soon have
constructed a vast history of, well, your own.
Still, for a civilization of one
its anatomy is just as real as you
were when I touched you, entered, reemerged.

This, then, is the power of knowing, this death.
When the last Krypton night simmers over
the rim of your world, when we meet in the sky
to find ourselves sharing stars, when what was
once familiar slinks away, disoriented,
hungry for the next clarity, remember

shadows cast from nothing in the dark.

On Jephthah

On my planet we read books. Our own.
Others'. Little, it is said, escapes
us. Your people have a story,
of Jephthah, the Gileadite. You claim
him unwilling conscience to the carnage
in his blood, his people's. Now what this meant
to your Hebrews—this sacrificial pact
a man made with an often arbitrary
God, the promising up of first meat,
of the first active soul across his
threshold to deitary hunger (this,
the deepest cut your story gives),
the accidental indenture of his only
daughter—what this meant, in exchange for luck
in battle, I have only the vaguest clue.

But from where I stand, from this rock
soon to be but little more than just
that, I can only console one father's
agony with my own. This world, Krypton,
is our child. We, each, may claim the flesh
of each, those pudgy portmanteaus
of skin, cloth, bone, our progeny…. Yes.
But then, the upshot of all this sex—
the waves we make, riding out the last
few evenings only indescribably
close to being alone, even all those
years of more (at least apparently)
significant evenings, meetings,
falling silk and fallen forms writhing
to indistinguish self from seed—all
of this is nothing I can tell you of.

What we have made, we have not made
permanent enough. It is not the child,
not that child's child, not me or the son
I have sacrificed so long before
the others, not my wife, nor her mother,
not her father's long parables
involving light and moving bodies—
it is not the simple loss of all this
which I share with your Gileadite,
but rather that of our true child, the only
begotten fragment of a fragmentary
sun. This *world* is what I offer
to the stars. *It* came, as it came to all
of us here, first. Moving out, breaching
my mother, her lap, that dark and bloody

threshold, *it* greeted *me*. Krypton crossed
then, equally from my perspective,
over into *my* dooryard. And now—
child or no, tambourine or no, menorah
or nothing but a fading yellow star—
we, these people of whom I am one
and whom I, in my decline, choose
to readopt through Jephthah, we, I....
Oh, my planetary daughter, we may
not understand this calamity you
have brought for us to witness, yet
we recognize the hand by which one points,
one claims, seizing the right to perish
in your name.

The Else

I can only imagine you from your attempts
at God, your artful mediation. From the swell
of that little mustachioed man (those first wartime
broadcasts full of hoops and ladders) to the greenswards
of your word wardens (the *else* they add to each rose
patterned web woven between worlds, the clapboards

of your inadequacies)—from then till now I have heard,
read, translated till my eyes are blue. I know you,
your languages, the irreconcilable
vacuum you imagine between what you say
and what you mean. Not that sublime absence out here,
between what you know and what you imagine I must

imagine, having, unlike you (at least till now) corresponded
with clusters, the sisters, a small turquoise planet
in the system you call Vega. No, this is what we were
made for, it turns out, this joining. Think of your own
roots, the slow ages of ozone, oxygen
and carbon learning to share a common bond.

Single cells wanting company, hot to trot
(you might once have said). For what? The agony,
really, of sharing. Across that data landscape,
from the first primordial actions of those prime
independent agents, from excitation
to inhibition, from precondition to Postman,

from worm to Wall Street to the Winnebagos
you've set adrift among the stars, you can trace the pattern,
the long way back to some sub-Saharan mountain. And if
you *have* begun to see us, this connection we've made,
as the same sort of least resistance, as the network
as it might have been, you might also have glimpsed the brain

we were meant to pick, the vast challenge of galactic
consciousness, infinite confusion. But then all this
is moot, nothing more than a hardening
of the arteries, a misremembering, glitch,
a brush with lips whose sordid braille you missed the chance
to read. Knowing (as you will) that there is no more,

that this sector must at last grow mute, that its promise
will speak now only to the unfinished, will you still want
me to have come at all? Or will you, wishing to have looked
elsewhere when searching, make just enough mistakes
to find me, to smell again the smell of your first rain,
supposing that nothing which happens subsides?

JHVH

Is this my world, or yours? It is hard,
with so much information, to keep track
these days of just whose flesh is whose.
I read about an upstart, a ten-year-old,
in your papers. *Summa cum laude*, Bachelor
of Arts. He said, "Finally," as he crossed the stage.

And then there was that plane somewhere over
the Caucasus. No hydraulic fluid.
So they emptied jugs of lemonade
into the lines. When they landed, the pilot,
an atheist, crossed himself and took off
his left shoe. Of that corpse that caught fire

in bed, in its coffin (in Ohio,
maybe Athens), authorities said, "We blame
the embalmer. Or the weather." Your Pope
has named genetic engineering sin.
Yet doesn't even Host begin as wheat,
human intervention? Such are the mysteries

of your age…. A man born without shoulders
offers to brave a well, reclaim another's child.
A faceless figure in China stands down
a tank. A woman in New York, riding
an escalator, falls through. It grinds her
under heels of those who stare, untrampled.

In Tunguska, some decades ago, some *Thing*
exploded. The trees splayed out like sticks.
It left no crater. When poisoning rocked
the rule of Louis XIV, more than three
hundred nobles were tried for sorcery,
for soaking each other's shirts in arsenic.

Banning fortune-tellers, putting a lid
on the sale of poison, Louis declared
witchcraft a superstition, denied
the existence of any trial, failed
to finesse the record. You look for reason
in the strangest places. For God. For proofs

against. You accumulate accidents,
incidental information, a piece
of rose china here, a political
theory there. You connect, create, slather
layer on layer, ignoring the strain
of the weight of it all and, *some*body's god

willing, escape before the structure sees
collapse. It is easy to dismantle
prevailing sentiments. Easier though
to find joy, at last, confronting the sublime,
to suspect, when disruption knocks,
an ampleness, opportunity.

Some time from now, in the early morning,
perhaps a late, lazy, autumn afternoon,
your astronomers will record the first sign
of nonhuman, off-world intelligence.
A message. Perhaps this.
I can only imagine.

The Mysteries of Azazel

What if I told you your gods were dead,
and where to find the bodies?
Named some Vatican vault, a tomb in Siam,
a rock-throated grotto
in Venezuela so deep you can see stars
at day? Told you the tale
the Anasazi tell of their leaving?
Explained Roanoke,

North Carolina, its vanished colony, the sign
that read CROATOAN?
Untangled the tasty fate of Earhart? Egypt's
thirty-second dynasty?
DNA perhaps? The alphabet of the Grail,
the asymptotic parameters
of the Rosy Cross? How long before Π
becomes regular? When earthquakes?

Why whalesong? Leaf-cutter ants—what's their grammar,
their recipe for kohlrabi
stew? Maybe Buddha? His bones? The first novel
of Lao Tzu? Where *this* Quetzalcoatl,
that raft of snakes, this Ark, the next quark
pair? I could talk to you
about Schrödinger, calm your insecurity
about his cat. Tell you why angels.

Why not mind mites or temporal restrictions.
We have studied you, you
know. Know more than maybe you do yourselves.
I say *maybe. Perhaps.*
It is this word that makes me curious.
Do you understand more
by not knowing? Would you believe that if

you dug half an inch down,
just under the first, crisp, re-entry layer
of the Ka'ba stone's skin,
there you'd find a titanium screw?
Titanium no one's seen
before, unlikely, full of promise? How
about Flight 19,
those fighter planes of yours, or the herb
sequence to animate

a golem? I could tell you anything.
I am alien. First
contact. There are advantages to speaking
first…across time. I am dead
after all. Yet my eyes have been others.
When I knew our doom,
I began sharing yours. I have lived this
way, with your lives. I've seen priests,

Punjabi, parochial teachers, the odd sparrow
fall. So, the way to the river
Lethe then? The golden city of Ubar? No, like Troy,
that one's done for. Then how
about the dark night of the soul, its quantum
mechanical effect?
Or the name of the man on the grassy knoll?
His present occupation?

Or what if I gave you a graven stone?
Just that, for all this absence.

The Curse of the Pharaohs

My son will be your Moses. He came from a red sea.
Crossing the dark channel between folds between worlds,
he will arrive through the open maw of that jewel-toothed gulf
articulate, astute, uncanny for his age, able
to leap tall buildings in a single bound. It is this last,

though, which will eventually, troublingly, bind him.
What limits can one legislate for him, who is his own
(and only) legislation? Thus, he will have to keep close
counsel. Talk to himself even. Try to speak to the burning
alone, from some high precipice. They are always high.

And, unimprisoned by you, freed on account of the madness
in your hearts, for the purpose of breaking the laws you need him
to
maintain, he will, like some gusty god-king, have power over you,
and he will bruise your heel. And there will be enmity
between what he stands for and what he accomplishes

in your midst. And, more than likely, you won't recognize
this, the synchrony of it, not any more than those harried
Hebrew wanderers noticed—passing under Job's coffin,
the heel of Hercules perhaps, or Venus, or the serpent
Hydra—how, just then, my only son was passing through.

The Secret Diaries of Lois Lane

*...nothing less than a bursting shell
could penetrate his skin.*

—Jerome Siegel & Joe Shuster
Action Comics, 1938

Man or Superman

I've often heard that every woman wants
one, a Superman to carry her
away. Some singularly divine fellow,
the kind one only meets in movies, alien
to the ways of your average lout.
Imagine Oz. Thor without the thunder.
But what if he knows too much to begin
with, the color of your underwear perhaps?

Or the secret slouch of your breasts, the hang
dog puckers under makeup under eyes
he can read even the *names* of drinks in?
Or suppose further. He doesn't mind.
Remember, your lover won't grow
crow's feet, those whose murderous caws
you've already been hearing for the past
(what?) two years. And when even these begin

to fade, giving way to the kind of embrace
he will surely pity, will you wonder
what he may have seen growing inside
you? What death he may have burned away,
what left behind? What expectation
he may have infected with his own? Will
you hate him then? Or, like some brave new world's
new Magdalene, will you cast away your old

devils, leave him, rise?

Give to Her Your Cloak Also

I understand the necessary lie,
that pasty face he passes off for work,
the interest vested in his paper
tiger. But, frankly, three in a bed
is not what I had planned. Each night
that I slip—calling him, from some stark peak
of passion, Clark—the covers grow more
crowded, the issue, more cumulous.

To which side do I cleave then? On which
thunderous thigh do these nails leave
no trace? Though there are times I enjoy
such naughtiness (the occasional
quick one in Perry's office, a hot kiss
on the fly), I still find it hard
to divide time between what he is
and what he's had to hide to be just

that. Don't get me wrong, Diary, I love
the both of him, but these days, when I send
him out for squeeze cheese and chips, when
he comes back, Midway Mart sack in one
hand, would-be thug in the other, I can't
help wondering…. Should I prefer this
Superman who saves a world a week,
or he who's learned to live his life

by loaning it his cheek?

Orgasm Over Mt. Ararat

I don't suppose our stars are crossed
on quite the same axis as others'. His, rather
red—mine, yellow. It's a wonder when we fuck
in flight we don't go nova. But that's just it,
isn't it? Love's not about how well we fit
the other's holes. Nor who's got the balls,
or wears the pants, or claims the panty
fetish. That gender stuff breaks down too handily.

No, no matter how alien he may be,
we both began the same. Furrier perhaps.
Lungless even, when we scaled the face of the deep
and, before that, the space between stars—our matter
identical, our evolution parallel.
We both started, for example, with vaginas.
So all that star stuff, what I call the horrible
scope, is no more helpful than religion.

Look at David and Bathsheba, David
and Jonathan, Bathsheba and her maid....
No one can tell you just *who* you may claim
for eternity. When that young Babylonian
couple arrived at the top of their mountain,
equal and alone, when Utnapishtim turned
to his bride, promising her the Flood
was done, I bet she jumped his bones. This is how

we fly. Bumper to bumper. Backseat to the sky.

His Maculate Erection

Making love to Superman comes easy,
Diary, like riding a perpetual bike.
Considering the contents of his genes,
though, that's another game entirely.
Imagine, for example, his super sperm.
Do those tiny, whipping tails ever flag?
Do they remain inside, set up shop, waiting
for my tubes to, miraculously, retie?

If we play at soap and wandering hands,
if he christens me indiscriminately
in the shower, should we try to plug the drain?
I invent the most frightening scenarios.
There, in the dregs of that porcelain dark,
following raveling threads of sewer,
a billion souped up cells continue to swim,
blind and eternal, toward the light.

And when the water turns again—past
its requisite recycling plant—back
into some home, innocent, silent, two baths
(probably the suburbs), how will that housewife
explain? I can see her face, her frustration,
all the excuses her long-fixed husband will see
as feeble. Some months from now, maybe a year,
familiar tales will be retold, all the old

fables recycled.

That Mermaid Again?

Even Atlantis has to have its vamps.
Since he told me about her, that mermaid,
months ago—about Lori Lamaris, the ex
siren unsurfaced from his past—since then
I've begun, writer that I am, to fabricate
her life. When I imagine myself, sans legs,
curling the wide arc of my rippled flank
through breaker, over riptide, under living

arches of coral and down to my secret
home, I allow myself to curse her.
And admire her. And take her voice, returning
what Andersen, one Hans Christian, stripped
away. I understand. I know. See, my lover
can fly. And though I've had my day
on a Concord or two, though I've fended
off more than your average number

of lowlifes, I can only see through walls
as well as lead. And I've never really gotten
to the bottom of any ocean. Should I blame
my love then? Or those like Hans who deny my soul,
maintaining a need to marry first—to attach
my reach to that of some prick—so testosterone,
somehow holy, can earn for me my entrance
into heaven? Success aside, I still get lost

in Atlantis, that fluted tale, knowing I'd trade nothing for the ride.

The Wedding Party

Speaking of marriage, I hear his mother
wants me to make an honest man of him.
He laughs at this, his parents' quaint Kansasisms.
But what *would* we do, Diary, honeymoon
on the moon, maybe at that fortress of his
up north, make love under a sky gone mad
with color? And just whom would we invite?
The last few Kryptonian citizens

he keeps corked up in a bottle somewhere?
Supergirl? Krypto, that mutt with super
dog breath? Maybe the members of Justice
League, the Legion, his younger, alternate self?
Oh God, and the party-crashers. Swamp Thing,
Solomon Grundy. *Do you think, Honey,*
I'd ask him, *the Black Canary might warble
a tune or two?* Really, this is serious.

We have no friends (at least not typical,
mortal) whom we could dare endanger.
And how should I prepare? Rice, zinnias,
a slug of anti-kryptonite in my shoe?
Like one of those virgins I used to study
in the Gospels, should I trim my lamp,
prepare for the Bridegroom's uncertain coming?
Or is that long dead world's Last Son

impervious to my burning?

Necropolis

This city, for him, is only a fair
weather fantasy. He knows nothing of death
but the anecdotal. His dreams—I know
he has them—speak not to that which drives
the rest of us to build the monuments
we do. When we flew into New Orleans,
for example, Florence, Nazlett El-Sese
in Egypt, when we read of the latter—

how some dig had dug up the final
secret (the Great Pyramid's construction),
found an ancient harbor that licked and lapped
papyrus plant, once, near the paps of the Sphinx,
how Cheops must have shipped quarried stone there,
where slaves muscled its many tons from less
distance than we'd thought before—he shook
his head, disgusted at what he could not see

as anything but wasted life. Canopic
jars too, those many-headed urns jammed
with the body's imperfect jewels, mummies,
the urge for children even, the pagan plates
adopted by Rome and traded up for tombstones....
Nothing which touches the afterlife
touches him. I wonder what he'll do then
when I'm gone. Or Jimmy. Lana. Perry. All

Metropolis? How will it be, this haunted glass necropolis?

Lex Luthor's Complaint

Letters from Arkham Asylum

You cannot touch my planet without destroy-ing something precious.

— Superman, in *The Dark Knight Returns*
Frank Miller, 1986

Midrash

Should I lift a leaf from Lovecraft, from Poe?
Explain, oh-so-lucidly, just what sort
of mad I'm not? Tell you all the gorgeous
things I've done were done for my father's sake,
that he beat me when I shaved the cat, bolted
it to a plank of balsa wood and shot it
through with ions till it spoke? My parents
don't exist. Should I mention that too? The I.
R.S., Customs, Social Security,
the Census Bureau—none of them have records
anymore. I was six when I managed it,
and, though secretly astonished, they punished
me then as well. So I guess I should tell you
how I *do* believe in law, in jurisprudence.
Not in spite of what I've done, but *because*.

The tsunami I whipped up from nothing
back in '78; the hordes of armed
fruit bats who rampaged through the better
part of Metropolis for forty days
and nights; the various forms of techno-
voodoo, hypnosis, cryogenic stasis
I have visited upon one Lois
Lane these many years; the stock market
burps, crashes (both bull market and bear);
all the lionizing I have, quite
unintentionally, directed Superman's
way was meant to mean one thing, one only.
My life, all that I have done, the sentence
I'm now serving, is precisely that:
serving. Not myself, but you, the law.

It's Superman who's broken the social
contract. Mr. Hup-Two-Three, Mr. Big
Cheese in Primary Colors Man. Blowhard.
You move at his every beck, come to his
every call, dream in line with whatever
aliens dream, and—too like that Biblical
king, Nebuchadnezzar—mistake the myth
for the message. You *are* the great tree,
the statue with feet of crippled, cracked tarmac,
and he, he is the cobbled stone you've thrown
only at yourselves. He cannot stand
for what he must, by definition, break.
So I must break him for you. Be assured,
while I am here, grazing on grass and locust,
scapegoated to this wilderness, unclean,

cast out, my thoughts are ever with you
and never far from he who put me here.
He will destroy you with his false trinity,
those angry colors he wears. And the rainbow
you see, rising up from the devastation
of order you've tried so hard to cultivate,
will only last as long as he needs you
to serve his final longing, his heaven
brought down to earth. Krypton, I've heard,
was barren at the end. Do not mistake
his purpose. Though you may not believe
it now, already he has bruised your heel,
already he goes to prepare a plot
for you, a final potter's field. What the Man
of Steel has stolen from you is not

purely Occidental.

Methuselah

I grow old. Like a rabbi long on Torah
and short on immanence, like some Pharisee
too intent on keeping his temple intact,
I *do* grow old in this gothic greystone,
plotting how to line my palms, his casket,
each imagined cloud, with silver. *Superman.*
Can I go a day without that thug's thorny name
rising up from the stones about me? The others
here, the real loons, they fairly worship him.
Some claim they saw his star fall. No matter
that he (well, he and Batguy) put them here.

Once upon a time, crime was simple. A thief
reaped what he did not sow. Now, what with God
awake in the garden, a good capitalist
(one with head enough for three on his shoulders)
can't even heist an apple without crossing
Yahweh on the way to that other tree—of life.
The gates that give on justice have grown crowded,
packed with polyester rats, too many
in far too little space. They eat their young
on the run between Manhattans (added onions),
luncheons, and benefit backgammon games.

Even these, though, I stomached once. I knew
how to grease their whiskers. Superman
is another story. Armani isn't
his style, and women…well, he always had
the best already. The kingdoms of the Earth,
bread, a little peace and quiet—these are not
mine to offer. All I know is how I must
have been born too late, too perfect *not* to
foil. Still, plans are ever legion, and as long
as we're a country where Reagan once wept, crept

41

crepuscular, where Give-Em-Hell-Harry settled
on settling the East with crematorium
shadows; as long as this remains the place
where Washington longed to face the dollar
with himself, his entourage, a column
of fire; as long as the incommensurate
moments still come and go, like the burning
of Yellowstone or Challenger's bright, brief
spark, I know we won't at last succumb
to him, to the chaos his order implies.
Instead, when I am even older yet—my hands
no longer heavy with his restraining

clause—I will show my grandchildren a torn
cape, some singed tights, and watch them shrink, point,
adorn me with aahs. Only then will I suffer
the interest of children. *Come to me*, I might
say, *trace my tracks, my crow cracks, the long ladder*
each scar has become. He thought he was eternal,
but he couldn't grow old.

The Model

—On keeping busy in the madhouse

First, you must collect the unfamiliar
pieces, this dither, toward a central hub.
Do not, though, mistake pretended order
for any eventual imposition
of form: Albatros, Stuka, Fokker.
Gathering what remaining supports you
find—those whose barely-molded planes suggest
horizons—along the end of the space
you've cleared away for your endeavor,
it should be readily apparent which
boundaries you will need. Small parts, recall,
do not imply lesser helpings of discontent,
though they may provoke less delicate
profanities. Can you live (you may be
imagining) with the occasional
prop, shock, spring you've left behind? Early on,
one should watch for false fits that merely seem
expedient. You will need every throttle,
each ambiguous strut, to fill the space
you've vacated for a final version.

Maybe it's not even an airplane,
this craft begun from your departure.
Try not to fret over the wing you mistook
for a stand, the stand you may yet take
for simple ornament; at least the choke
will probably turn out right. Remember,
camouflage hides even the most damaging
evidence of shoddy work. Only
in certain stages is a flush juncture
of, say, hull and hindquarter demanded.

Ruptures along the seams will appear
insubstantial in context—figments even—
with, of course, enough glue. Now, though the primer
you have chosen (its mysterious fumes)
may elicit discussions of vanishing,
though the smell of apples, as it builds
up, is evidence of your mounting
success, though you kind of like the heady
sacrifice such bold exposure permits,
you must account for moderation.

Dote on Wonder Woman now and then,
on her generic, see-through bomber, on how,
in her world, the real McCoy—a B-29,
C-130—must ever be thought transparent.
Following stratagems need to trouble
the potential for failure in any image
you itch to construct of martyrdom.
The blueprints provided for your venture
are, after all, not to be taken
for granted. And though color diagrams
may prove falsely accessible by virtue
of their seeming lack of art, please be assured
you *can* do this. Isn't *this* the vague
rationale that instruction, by definition,
proclaims? Even in another tongue,
the directions model you in future
tense, allowing that you will, at last, finish
construction, that you will need such final steps—
an outline—when you arrive there, moving
still, projecting, on to your completion.

The Dark Knight of the Soul

is awake as I'm awake, here in Gotham.
Darkly dressed, figmentary, he doesn't bind
against my brain the way Superman is wont.
No, though Batman too skulks the streets, fighting
crime with crime, at least bats make no bones
about hypocrisy. There is acknowledgment
in his very hood—that velvet job with ears
that could be horns, horns that could be emblems
of the devil he denounces even as he serves.

The thing about bats is their adaptation—
each hand grown large, fingers extended, curved
into brittle ribs. And then, the way they've learned
at last to see inside the caul that calls them
out to feed—sonar. Dark shapes bounced back
for capture in those creepy, crass containers
balanced at the axis of each skull. These ears,
it appears, tack them to our terror
spots, invest them with the vestments of night.

They eat mosquitoes, rid us of parasites,
help cleanse our evenings of plague. For just
such gifts, we fear them. What makes one handy,
then, of use in this world, can also make one
horrible. And this, I argue, this—on nights
when I cannot sleep for the sound of two kinds
of flight alight in the heart of our city's sole
darkness—this is how it *should* be.

Inscription for an Asylum

What lack, the perimeter of our knowing,
what taste, the purchase of that lapse,
what guile, our denial of absence owing
to minds that muster might from each perhaps.
—Dr. Amadeus Arkham, 1921

The loons who run the halls here—ever ravished
by a moon that makes odd promises to wed them—
they come to me, and pray, and they are lavished
with my own hysteric offerings of bedlam.

This house was meant to loom a little larger
than the others down these streets of stucco crypts.
But *all* my neighbors—lunatic to barber—
accept this stuffy Superman, his rise and his eclipse,

as if he weren't the golden calf he is.
If *Moses* couldn't brave the face of Jealousy,
who are we to lend a God our eyes?
If all we ever see are but the buttocks of eternity,

if, when the law is handed down, *all* tablets
must break, if what some Hubble sees is a mistake
of taking, too patently, the blueprints
for a universe we'd rather frame than fake,

if even part of this is true and yet you let
proclaimed perfection in a red cape rule you,
something (sanity) there is that you forget:
Rest at the cost of another's rod can fool you.

Thus, the plaque that meets your eye upon the brace
beside this door—the motto that's inscribed here,
Doctor Arkham's only warning—should face
the faces yet within. If entering, beware.

46

Some Jokes

I.

Two guys standing on a roof in Metropolis.
One says to the other, "I bet I can leap this
rail in a single bound...not get hurt. Wind'll blow
me back like a boomerang." The second fellow,
not to be outdone, takes him up on the wager,
pulls out a sawbuck, lays it on the rail, says, "Sure."

So the first guy straightens his tie, fingers the fall
breeze—an old salt testing his sea—and does a cannonball
over the ledge. Minutes later, winded, he comes back
just long enough to snag his stakes. Two other saps,
watching slack-jawed from across that great, gaping lack
between buildings, see this. Says one to his friend, "Fuck!

Is that guy lucky or what?" His companion passes
it off with a shrug: "That's just Superman in glasses
and a bad suit. How did you *think* he made a living?
Cracking hard cases, occasional skulls, rescuing
every kid, cat, careering train that runs away?"
You know, folks, I ask myself this same thing, every day.

II.

Peter at the pearly gates, shifting from wing tip
to wing tip. When, out for a stroll, Jesus passes, quips,
"Tough job," his favorite ex-apostle (only human),
he who's needed a bathroom break for a millennium,
asks his Rabbi to stand in for a spell. Jesus,
welcoming a new perspective on all this bliss,

says sure. So Peter shows him what to do. "Just
ask a few questions, cross-reference their answers the best
you can with the concordance here. Make certain you stamp
their hands." Some little while later, an old man walks up.
Jesus asks him his name. "In your language? Joseph."
Occupation in the last life? "Carpenter." A brief

recognition begins to cross Christ's mind. He asks him
if he had any children down below. "One. A shame
he wasn't born normally—he came from a star."
Jesus, really suspicious now, asks, "Did he differ
that much from other boys?" The old man nods.
"He wasn't always human, had a voice like God's

that followed him, guided his ways." Jesus, almost
agog now, says, "You loved him." The geriatric ghost
smiles: "He came to me in answer to my prayers."
Elated, Christ asks, "Did he have any marks, scars?"
"Well," the elder offers, "he had nails in his hands...."
"Father!" exclaims Jesus. "Pinocchio!" cries the man.

     III.

Okay, let's see if I can clear this up. The joke's
on us. We think what we want is Law, primal spokes
on a wheel of cosmic order. What we forget is how
wheels turn, evolve, shift as we shift, restless now
in our rumble seats. We neglect, in the rush to solve
our rat problem, the potential mongoose breeding curve.

Do we really want a savior who will know *every* fall,
hear *each* sparrow's plumeless plummet? This rare bull
we've loosed amongst what only *seems* perpetual—
amongst an inventory of arbitrary rules fragile
as china—is not the Mithra we think he is. We mistake
corrective power for correction. He's no fake

(would that it were that simple), but neither is he Christ
or the Lady in the Lake. The Word made flesh? Worst
case scenario. The Law itself? He can't evolve.
No, the paradigms we build, we build to solve
human equations. Stasis, what his steel jaw suggests,
is only as eternal as our last, best jests.

Through a Glass, Darkly

...for the letter of the law killeth,
but the spirit giveth life.
          —II Corinthians 3:6

It was a lovely paperweight, that Bible
Mother used to read me my own mythology
from. She called it a heritage of truth,
named it namable, translatable, steady
as the morning star, saw its message
in the present tense, unwavering, apt.

Though she learned these readings from a suit
some pulpit had ordained, though his ordination
was itself an act of faith, for her, words meant
something we could apprehend. They did not
change, call for interpretation. *For now*
we see through a glass, darkly was clear to her.

Me, I want to know what *for now* suggests.
Is it *thus* now, or *just* for now, now *only*?
And while we're at it, who the hell is *we*?
Paul and his cohorts? The *in* Christians?
Perhaps the Corinthians he's addressing.
But the Jews too? Everyone? Or only

the saved? Then there's this wily little verb, *see*.
See has a long and lustrous tradition
of obfuscation. The first definition:
a seat, a throne, the rank symbolized
by all such butt-rests of authority; the chair
of a bishop, the Church itself, a cathedral

or office of the Pope. Second meaning:
a glance. Third, from the Old English *seon*,
Old Frisian *sia*, Old Norse *séa*: to perceive
with the eye an external object, to become
aware of (in the mind's eye) as in a dream
or vision; perhaps to distinguish

by sight *from* some similar object, to attain
comprehension of, understand, foresee;
to forecast, have a particular mental view
of, appreciate or recognize or believe;
to accept, contemplate, examine, visit;
to know, to be a willing witness, watch

over, take care of, ensure through supervision;
to judge. Which, I ask, will it be? There are more,
to be sure—several shaky columns
in the trusty O.E.D.—but then we must
remember, these are *English* variants,
not the original Greek. What might

Longinus have seen in the word, that scholar
of the sublime? Moving on, it gets even
trickier. *Through*. Is this to be taken
in the instrumental sense? By means of?
Or shall we infer the local, more simple
sense: *through* a glass? Preposition, nothing

more. What then of this *glass* itself? Are we
talking a window here? I understand
their panes were made of mica back then.
Hard, I imagine, to see through. So vision,
Paul says, is inherently impaired—the world
outside, a grainy, imperfect substitute

for the real, the ineffable probably
already before us. Something we can't,
with mortal discretion, judge. But this assumes
too much. *Glass*, for the Elizabethans
(this version comes, after all, from the days
when Shakespeare had not yet bequeathed his wife

their second-best bed), *glass*, for King James' crowd,
did not have to be transparent. The word,
for them, meant also and more properly
a mirror. So we see *as through a mirror*.
Wait a minute. Let's be confused *together*
for a while. How does one see *through* such

a thing? One doesn't. One sees what is behind,
the hinder portions of God perhaps, the back
water regions of ourselves, our history,
the shadow in the corner of some Corinthian
hut, what we never were, what the world
might be if we could spin on one heel

fast enough. But, as always, by the time
we turn, it's gone. Whatever *it* was. Then is
this just another version, a prefiguring
if you will, of that famous Alice, of her own
linguistic confusion? She, too, had to play
hide-and-seek with a mantel full of babble.

Finally, then, we come to *darkly*.
Mirrors, the most ancient ones, were imperfectly
polished metal, the reflections they managed,
obscure. *Darkly* may suggest this. Paul
may mean that what we see, we see obscurely,
as if *through* mica or *in* a mirror.

But might not he also be speaking
to that which we perceive, *always*, darkly,
glass or no? The glass, then, not *glass* but flesh?
Our eyes themselves? The perception we adopt
of seeing? I could linger on the modern
schematics of how eyes really work—the world

coming to us, as it does, upside down—
how image is only that, an image,
and discuss the implications (what even
Goethe troubled himself over) of light,
because, well…. See, things have no color,
only properties of absorption, reflection,

and…. But perhaps more to the point, *darkly*,
literally and in the Koine dialect,
is not *darkly* at all. James' boys took
certain liberties. The Pauline version
reads ἐν αἰνίγματι, for the layman,
in an enigma. We could read this, then,

adverbially, as in: *for now we see*
through a glass, enigmatically. But back
when we were still stealing enough ambiguity
to make our language interesting, *darkly*
probably worked better, had more charm,
less clarity, more, well, enigma

in and of itself. God, in the Septuagint,
uses the same word referring to Moses:
"With him will I speak mouth to mouth, even
apparently, and not in *dark sayings*."
Here, the enigma is still dark—our translators
preferring poetry to what we might

call pure—but the question is, can the Word
be pure? Should it? New Covenant or old,
King James, Living, Revised, New English,
Jerusalem? The versions of versions revised
through each dark seeing, translated through eyes
and on to brains where hearts, more than hands,

take over.... Well, isn't the point of Christ's
coming a return of power to each of us,
each woman and man who might not even have
seen the temple curtain tearing? Incarnation
validates the holiness of perspective, each
vessel, each glass, this limited, lush

glory of confusion. This is what we are.
Not supermen, not perfection dressed
in our garish, red, blue and yellow Sunday
best. We, the world we read, are Torah.
Superman, the constancy of his concupiscent star,
is less than this. A big red S. A text

we read too lightly.